# I Aim to Misbehave
## (Why is my fingers red?)

*By Curtis R. Crim, BA CEO*

ISBN: 978-0-9833732-5-4

Printed in the United States of America

First Printing

# Dedication

This book is lovingly dedicated to Nellie,
Joy of My Life, and mother of my children.

## AND

Sarah Silverman, for being the prettiest,
cutest, hottest, smartest, sexiest and the
cleverest comedian of all time!

# TABLE OF CONTENTS

# Disclaimer 1

My humor tends to be a bit edgy at times, so I strongly suggest that anyone with a weak stomach not proceed. If you do, take all necessary precautions, such as putting on your adult-sized diapers, and making an airsick bag handy. No matter whether you find my jokes sickening or unbearably funny, it is better to be safe than sorry.

# Preface: One Crazy Fucker

I will stipulate to being insane. It is not like I fail to function in society, but I see the world differently from the way humans see it.

Because of my unique view of the universe, reality and culture, my consciousness is free to surf the cosmos unrestrained by proprieties, expectations, tradition, and pressure from other people's perspectives.

This has often been a disadvantage in life. Being different from everyone else frequently provokes persecution and prejudice. But then, if one can't laugh at this world, one's existence is destined to be mostly wasted.

Being unrestrained by societal manipulation and brainwashing sometimes leads me to envision scenarios that most people's consciousness and subconscious would normally edit out.

I hope that you are entertained by my humor, and that your mind's boundaries are expanded in an amusing fashion.

**Additional Disclaimer**: Be warned that reading the following material could have an adverse effect on your psychology.

Therefore, any negative impact of my jokes upon your mind is purely your legal responsibility. I disclaim any responsibility for fucking your mind up if you read beyond this point. You have been warned.

# Introduction:
# The Purpose of this Book

I have been a clown all of my life. I started joking with my mother before I could walk or talk. When I got to elementary school, I was the class idiot who would eat paper and napkins just to make the other children laugh. My father was also a big fan of puns and joking. When I got to college, I was able to make entire classrooms of students literally fall out of their chairs and roll on the floor laughing with my unexpected and inappropriate comments about the Maharishi and the things he said.

Being funny appears to be a talent which a have naturally.

My goal in writing this book is not to write the funniest book or the funniest jokes of all time. It is also not to write the most gross, disgusting or vile jokes and mind trips of all time. However, keep in mind that many of my jokes are inclined towards dirty humor, and I go over the line frequently. I believe that I have unintentionally succeeded at coming up with some of the most rude and offensive concepts and jokes ever, but this also came to me naturally and effortlessly.

Note that I am not going to focus in on grammar or spelling in this book, because of the comical context. Some of the words are misspelled intentionally to bring additional meanings into the joke.

The purpose of this book is simply to offer fresh new jokes and humor, which effortlessly come to me as I work on my organic farm. I experience a huge level of creativity, and I often hear jokes in my head as though I am the audience. Most of the jokes in this book came to me during the 2011 growing season. Enjoy!

# Chapter 1: One-Liners

Doesn't Tabouli sound like a food that you should not eat, and if you do, it is best to not talk about it?

Have you ever crapped your pants so hard that you had to change your shirt?

It shouldn't be NECESSARY to emasculate a woman.

Can a gay guy find sea men in a sailor's bar?

I am sorry, but TORTURE is a *terrible context* for a practical joke!

Why aren't white babies born with horns?

Why is it that when you try to fuck a bitch in the ass she has to be such a cunt about it?

The title of the movie, "In the Cut", is off by one letter.

Why do they call them the "right wing" when they are so against anyone having rights?

My definition of "precursery" is when I am warming up to say something really offensive!

I gal asked me what time it was, so I told her, "2:69".

"School" is where Iowans go to *not* learn anything!

What's the difference between a casserole and an asshole role?

I understand that many men don't even recognize the women they know if they only see their faces.

Do you ever grade your ass on performance?

If dogs controlled high technology, would they have shit cologne?

I *might* be a whore, but at least I'm no slut!

Spiders don't like being petted.

I'm so fuckin' hungry I could eat an asshole!

Chickens are cock-suckers!

Chicks blow off a pervert SO quickly; they don't even find out what you have to say!

Hypochondria must be lethal; in time, every hypochondriac dies.

I hear that a group of cats is a pride, where a group of dogs is just a fuckin' shame.

It takes a village to raise a village idiot!

I gave my cat a laxative and he crapped into dimensions of the universe that aren't even visible to human beings!

I like to clean the kitty litter box before breakfast, because it helps stimulate my appetite.

It's okay to play with your food... if you are a cat.

There are VERY few people whom I trust in this world, and they are ALL ME!

I've been baking for years, so hopefully I am ready to eat.

If you are a double amputee with no arms, you'll eat just about anything you can get your hands on…

Have you ever had a pet who you loved, and you licked its cunt?

Given the intelligence of the Human species, it is not a compliment to call someone the smartest person in history.

Do they make a human meat steak rub?

Is fucking a donkey considered ass-rape?

Little Red, Riding Robin Hood...

Why is it that when a woman looks up and away, you have NO CHOICE but to look at her breasts?

Have you ever been awakened by the feeling of diarrhea shooting out your asshole?

When a vampire goes down on his girlfriend, does he prefer it if she is having her period?

Has any culture made a sauce specifically to be eaten with long pig?

If your balls ARE a witch, do you have to burn them?

It is not necessarily bad if someone shits on you, depending on whether you are a seed.

I don't even need the internet; I already have kittens.

I am exactly like a billionaire, except that I have better morals, and less money.

There's nothing like Jewish war profiteer to inspire patriotism!

There IS no politically correct word for "lesbian".

Excuse me, waiter, but *I* placed a New World Order.

If there were cats up your ass, you would act crazy too!

If your main hobbit crashes, you get a backup hobbit...

What about a bull farm reminds one of how the average American citizen is treated by the billionaires these days?

People with Down's syndrome can't be pirates...

When I float around in a swimming pool, I feel like a turd floating in a toilet.

I take my cats very seriously; I take what they say kitty-litterally.

I think that **stalking** is the highest form of flattery.

If someone gave my sister a really strong laxative, her head would shoot right out of her ass!

Excuse me, but the head of my penis IS a brain!

Maybeline now makes a shit lipstick for fecalphiliacs.

I mean, of COURSE she despises and loathes me. It's part of being a woman. It's okay, though, because I fuck animals!

### Things to Never Do:

<This section contains some general guidelines which if followed might make your life more comfortable.>

Never eat your boogers on a first date.

Never wipe your butt with poison ivy leaves.

Never beat off right after you have been installing fiberglass insulation.

Never try to fuck a woman anally the first time you are having sex with her.

Never masturbate when you have poison ivy on your hands.

It might be cool to be omni these days, but here is a bit of advice: never try to rub yourself off on a cactus!

*Never* put an angry cat on your lap when you are naked.

# Chapter 2: Q & A Jokes

Question: Do you think that beating off is better than sex?
Answer: I dunno. It depends on WHO you're beating off!

Question: Why did the Maharishi cross the road?
Answer: He was being dragged by the fish hook through his cock!

Question: What do they call people who are on Facebook?
 Answer: Livestock.

Question: What's evil and comes in green?
Answer: Satan.

Question: If someone wants to FUCK a company's customers *and* employees, what do you call him?
Answer: An "administrator."

Question: What kind of a tree is a Country?
Answer: Peaches.

Question: What do you call a billionaire with a conscience?
Answer: Mythological

Question: What do you call a congressman who is not corrupt?
Answer 1: I have no idea. If you find one, we'll give it a name.
Answer 2: Extinct

Question: How many billionaires does it take to change a light bulb?
Answer: Just one to command his slave.

Question: What is the Japanese word for "Tsunami"?
Answer: Aaaaaaaaaaahhhh!!!

**Dead mother jokes:**

Question: Which tastes better, a dead mother or a dead aunt?
Answer: Don't worry about it. I ground the meat together.

Question: How many dead mothers does it take to change a light bulb?
Answer: I think you are going to have to change this one yourself, champ.

Question: What does Satan say after anally fucking your dead mother?
Answer: I'll let you know when he's done.

Question: How many dead mothers does it take to make love to an entire football team?

Answer: I'll let you know when they finish up and let me have the bodies back.

# Chapter 3: Puns

My girlfriend reminds me of my pussy cat. They both lap up the gravy as fast as I can squeeze it out of the package.

The other day, I heard a man yell "duck!" really loudly in the grocery store. I became very offended, because I didn't want my kids to hear any fowl language.

So these two guys were *literally* beating the crap out of each other! They were like, "Two shits that pass in the fight…"

# Chapter 4: Random Jokes

Have you ever woken up in the morning and noticed that two or three of your fingers have blood dried on them, and wondered what you did the night before?

What IS your national bird? I'm not sure... perhaps the dollar sign... or electricity...

I told the vet that I thought that my cat had worms, and he said for me to bring in a stool sample. It was an expensive test, and the results came back negative. Two days later I was thinking about it, and it occurred to me that he meant for me to bring in a stool sample from *my cat*.

I heard someone comment that yoga is a *form* of meditation. I think that's stretching the definition...

How about Assbook instead of Facebook? People could put nude pictures of their genitalia on their profile, and then boy would you see their "friends" numbers go RIGHT THROUGH THE ROOF!

If you are a dick and a potato, you are a dick-tater. Your kids are known as dictator tots.

Coach: There is no "I" in "TEAM".
Disgruntled team player: There is in "SUICIDE".

Being literate in Iowa is like being a hippie at a KKK rally. Perhaps you are not the minority that they are there to persecute, but you won't make any friends, and you had better not piss anyone off!

SUFI – Searching the Universe for Intelligence. Well, I started on Earth, but didn't find any. This is true, by the way: The people at SETI didn't bother searching the Earth for intelligent life, because they automatically assumed that they qualify!

The other day, this woman in the grocery store came up to me and said, "You sure are a big man."
"You said a mouthful right there." I replied.

Some people have a cross to bear, but I say *never* cross two bears, and further, it is very unlucky to come across two bears!

My IP address is my home address, because I don't like to go in public.

I am not a drunk, but I *am* a barracho. That's because I am only a lush in Spanish-speaking countries.

Why do they call it "Married", like it is in the past tense? Why don't they just say that you are Merry?

I stopped buying the extra sharp cheddar after I cut myself making a sandwich!

My dad used to boil down meat and make his own aspic. You know what they say; ass-pick is a matter of taste!

The best thing about being a brewer is that is the about the only vocation where you can go into work stoned off your ass drunk and still be able to create a great product!

Man to billionaire: "Do you like children?"
Billionaire: "Sure; they are very tender."

Woman: "Men get 100% of their brains from their mothers."
Man: "That's okay; most of us don't keep our intelligence there anyway."

In some places, heart attacks are illegal.
They are known as "Myocardial infractions".

Dude, there's a chink in your armor.
Yea, I know; that's left over from the tsunami.

Did you hear about this? Charlie Sheen initiated a law suit against Naomi Watts.

Then someone said to him, "Dude, they said *Tsunami,* not *sue Naomi.*"

There's this old crippled Japanese man with a bum leg and an arm missing from the war who was going through a garbage dumpster looking for discarded edible material. He has to forage in garbage for food, because he is considered untouchable and unemployable. He prays to God for something to eat. Just then, he looks up at the shore hearing a loud noise. He sees a giant wave coming towards the beach, and is quickly swept away along with everything and everyone in the area. As he drowns, he looks up at God and says, "I said *sushi*!"

Brainless Woman: "Men get 100% of their brains from their mothers."
Man: "Does that give each of your boys half a brain, or is the second one brainless?"

## GWB: The Great White Bastard

I don't think that George W Bush would do anything to stress out a horse. Not even HE is *that* heartless!

Even God is offended by the very NOTION of George W Bush!

What RACE of baby does George W Bush like to eat the most?

How do you know if a nigger belongs to George W. Bush? It has a "D" or an "R" next to its name.

I don't think that George W Bush could have drooled his way through one fucking jack-off without a lot of God damned help!

### Rednecks are Retards

*Cow*boy! What do you mean? His wife's a sheep.

If you have 3 kids all by different mothers, and are related by blood to each of the mothers, then you might be a redneck.

If you have had a kid with your sister and another with your daughter who was the result of that mating, then you might be a redneck.

Not ALL cowboys are gay. The OLD cowboys fuck livestock, where the YOUNG ones fuck each other.

### Farm Jokes

If a gal wants to turn on a man, she's going to do it; it doesn't matter what *species* she is. Do you think that a female sheep sometimes takes a shine to a farmer, and rubs her butt up against him in a feminine and seductive manner and in a sexy voice says, "Baaaaah"?

Does the sheep get jealous when you are fucking it, if you are *thinking* about fucking the pig?

Does the goat get jealous if you are thinking about a woman when you are screwing it in the ass?

When a farmer is fucking his pig, does he squeeze its ear and tell it to "squeal like Ned Beatty"?

Who came first, the chicken or the farmer?

A farm is heaven for a fecalphiliac. You can just run around naked smearing different kinds of shit on yourself. You can smell shit, eat shit and wear shit! You can even shove another animal's shit up your ass, then crap it out and have it for lunch.

I am an Iowan farmer, so my life revolves around bullshit and manure!

My chickens are Jews - they take Saturday off.

I call my baby chickens "chips" because they are chips off the old block. I call my adult chickens "chicks" because they are chicks off the old cock!

I don't have any ducks, so I got my chickens in a row.

It was the sheep's fault anyway; it was the way she was dressed!

I don't wear very much insect repellant - I naturally repel; it always worked on the girls in school!

One of my bee colonies is in a much angrier mood than the other one. I think it has to do with a scandal involving the queen.

Some people have ripped abs; well, I have ripped hands. It's from weeding.

If I can't get the weeds out of my garden, I might as well throw in the trowel and give up on it!

# Chapter 5: Dirty Jokes

Giving chickens away for free is like giving pussy away for free. You know that *someone out there* is either going to want to eat it, or use it for reproductive purposes!

I like cherries; I just prefer the pink ones to the red ones.

Before you say, "Lay it on Me.", be sure that the person you are talking to is *not* a fecalphiliac.

The cutest thing happened the other day: My mom and I farted at the exact same time! It was a total coincidence, and I will tell you how it happened. You see, I had just come in her asshole and pulled my cock out at the same time that my Aunt pulled her fist out of my butt. Ma and I butt queafed simultaneously. I then stopped licking my sister's tits and thought, "My God! I *am* becoming my father!"
Obviously, he was a very refined and sophisticated gentleman.

Can any of you lesbians tell me if, "Cat got your tongue?" means that it is harder to speak when you are eating pussy?

I *like* lesbians (or muffies, as I call them). I think that anyone who likes to eat pussy has great taste!

I love eating pussy so much that I'm an *honorary* lesbian!

No, no... There has to be a LOT more shit in my underwear before I figure that I've crapped myself!

CREW – A gang of gay guys is known as a "crew", which I think stands for, "Cornhole Repeated Entry Wound." It takes more than one man to commit gang rape, thus they are known as a "crew".

It's hard to play with too many kittens at once. Is it also hard to play with too many pussies at one time?

Some people "wouldn't hurt a fly." Well, I don't think that a fly is innocent. Do you know what a fly will do? It'll fly into your face a take a shit! Does that sound innocent? Anything that will shit *on your face* is NOT innocent! Well... I guess if it a woman who I **really** like...

Well, she might have been sucking dick, but she wasn't taking names!

Some jokes are known as skitty scatological; we know them as pussy jokes.

Girl: "...and I DON'T do anal!"
Man: "That's okay, baby; you just bend over and I'll take care of everything."

"I love your ass to pieces." I told my girlfriend. I also told her, "I love your asshole." She then asked me which it was: I love her ass whole or in pieces? And will she give you a "piece of ass" after YOU were the one who tore her asshole up?

I have always heard that you are what you eat, so I was quite surprised when a lesbian took offense because I called her a cunt.

There are animals whose assholes are normal to eat – like shrimp and oysters.

Do people sometimes know how your ass smells, just because they shook hands with you? Or that you fingered a pussy two knights ago?

Babies go through a stage where they are willing to put absolutely ANYTHING in their mouths. I bet over the ages there have been at least a few men who have taken advantage of that! Do you think that occasionally one of these guys decided to pull out at the very last second and just blow come all over the baby's face?

An aristocrat uses slaves to create a palate for shit art... He prescribes a different diet for each one because it produces crap with a specific color and texture for his paintings!

It is BETTER to think with your dick. Seriously! If you are a man and your brain works, you have that one thing working AGAINST you ever getting laid!

What do you mean, "Looking down at your tits"? My cock is looking UP at them!

I saw my cat sniffing his mom's butt from up close; his nose was almost touching his mommy's pussy. My only though I that I was glad that I never got my nose that close to my mother's ass! Well, not since I was born anyway...

Why do some people like to be shit and pissed on? I really don't get it... On the other hand, I guess it's warm, and some people might find that come-farting.

I was in the street in downtown Chicago when a prostitute approached me and said, "I'm celibate." I was obviously a bit confused by this, so I asked her, "How do you do your job?" (I meant no pun by the use of the word, "job"; it just *came* out that way...) She replied, "That *is* my job: Sell a mouth, sell a cunt, and sell a butt."

One thing that I have learned from my cats is that a pussy likes it when you pet it and play with it at the same time. ;)

If you want to get your wife pregnant, and you have balls but no cock, how do they make you ejaculate? How would they handle the matter if you were a bull on a bull farm?

Have you ever heard of Queen Ann's Lace? It is actually a weed (or an herb, but it's poisonous.) What I want to know is what Queen Ann did to get lace named after her. Lace is used in lots of lingerie. I am thinking that there were quite a few who sat on Queen Ann's face!

You have probably heard of the "five second" rule. If a piece of food drops on the floor and you can snatch it up right away, it is okay to eat it. Does that apply to other things, like perhaps a fork? Now, how about a fecalphiliac? If he is about to eat a turd and it drops on the floor, is it okay to eat if he picks it up fast enough? Well, what is he going to fucking say? "No, not *now*; it's DIRTY!"

# Chapter 6: Bits

## Human Anatomy

We are all familiar with standard human anatomy. But what if things had gone a little differently, and people were just put together slightly differently? How would have change our culture and how we interact with one another?

For instance, what if women had three or four sets of tits, like many other mammals do? (Most men have fantasized about this at some point) You could rub your balls against one set of tits while rubbing your cock on the set of tits next to them, and while fondling the set of tits closest to your hands, while at the same time you are kissing her lips (either set of them, that is.)

What if women had a pussy where their nose is? Could you have a conversation with a woman and be able to NOT stare at it? Or would you lean in to kiss her, and then stick your tongue in her face-cunt instead?

What if guys had a cock attached at the wrist instead of a hand? If two gay men were introduced to each other, everyone would know right away if they like each other!

What if men had ten dicks where they now have ten fingers on their hands? It sure would make a whole different experience for a young man feeling up a girlfriend for the first time!

What if women had a tongue right under their clitoris? Would they even bother leaving the house? And how cool it would be for a man who could have her lick your balls and cock at the same time you are fucking her? And it would make lesbian sex a HOLE different experience!

What if there was an asshole right between a woman's tits? I don't even have a punch line for this one. It was just a random thought generated by a demented mind.

What if a person had three sets of arms and hands instead of one? It sure would make masturbating more interesting! You could have yourself your own little orgy rather than just jacking off!

### What the FUCK *IS* Bajesus?

Have you ever heard the expression, "Scared the Bajesus right out of him!"?

What the heck is "Bajesus" anyway? It is obviously something that can be scared out of a person. Like shit.

Right after a near death experience, does a guy go to the bathroom and pull down his pants and say, "Jesus!"?

And what happens next...

The crap in his underwear looks up at him and says, "Yes, my son?"

### Edible Tampons

So let's say for a minute that they make edible tampons. Would it be assumed that they are going to include artificial flavors? Would one of those flavors be cherry? Or perhaps... pineapple? Would vampires love to eat the used ones?

### Anal Tongue Rape

You have certainly heard of the act of rape, and perhaps even ass-rape. But have you ever heard of someone tongue raping people's assholes? What if there was some pervert out there who likes to overpower smaller people and shove his tongue up his victim's ass? Can you imagine what it would be like to be made powerless and then have someone lick you asshole?

### Chicks Won't Date Me

Sadly, I can't have children. It's not that I am impotent... it's just that chicks won't date me!

Celibate does NOT mean that a woman is not going to have sex; it means that she is not going to have sex with ME. I have met many women who insist that they are celibate when I ask them out on a date, and within two years they are married with children and are pregnant on top of that. It turns out that for a woman to be celibate, she can have sex with as many people as she likes. Many women have claimed to me that they are celibate; I have learned that this only means that *I* am not going to get laid!

I actually used to buy this fucking "I'm celibate" line, until I realized that Fairfield, Iowa is like a fucking Mecca for lesbians. I used to actually think that women simply do not participate in sexual behavior, but I finally realized that it is not that they never have sex; it IS that they only have sex with each other. This is acceptable legally in Iowa. In Iowa, you can marry anyone or anything that you want. It's the cornholing capital of the world, right? You can marry a man or a woman; I think that you can even marry a goat. Fortunately for me, animals are far less discriminating than women!

You see, I give off this vibe to any woman who I think is sexy that I want to stick my cock in her mouth, her cunt, and her butt, and CHICKS HATE THAT! It's not my fault; call it a birth defect. I have very strong energy that is emitted by my dick, and women will literally fall down tripping over each other in some kind of stampede to avoid me!

I was once rejected by a lesbian who told me that she feels no attraction for me, but that she prefers to drink wine with her girlfriends in the evening. What do you think happens next? The pussy sex!

I am so totally envious of *anyone* who gets to have sex with a pussy! Jocks, lesbians - anyone who is fortunate enough to spend time with someone who has a vagina! Pussies are so beautiful and so special; and anyone born with a vagina is so exceptionally amazing and so special! I think that pussies are the most amazing thing on the planet! And yet I am the one man in a hundred thousand years who women will not have sex with for any reason!

I can even turn lesbians frigid towards each other just by walking into a room! Long ago, my friends learned to not invite me to parties, because when I walk in, every woman's libido turns to ice. Not only am *I* going to strike out (of course), but sadly no other guy at the party is going to get laid either if I have made a presence at the party. I am personally responsible for turning more women gay than anyone in history.

It is very hard to get a woman to go out on a date. Not for a lesbian, but for a man, it is nearly impossible. I have been asking women out on dates for about 35 years now, and have had little success at best. In spite of the fact that I live in the Midwest, women do not date fat men. Women also do not date old men, and if you are over thirty five years old, you automatically lose the interest of all young women and all of the cougars as well. However, the most crucial factor in getting a woman to say yes is self confidence. Do you know what most destroys self confidence? Rejection. The more you are rejected by women, the lower your self confidence becomes. I have even been rejected by a prostitute *after I paid her!* Now that's getting pretty bad. I have been pushed away by women since the mid 1970's. I have also had many women turn their face quickly away from me when I have leaned in to try to kiss them. If one has been rejected by women for decades, it will be very difficult to have any self confidence at all. I literally have virtually *no* chance of getting a woman to spend some time with me. It's okay, though; I fuck animals.

Lesbians are frequently skinny, and that totally turns me on! Many a woman has told me that she will not sleep with me because I was born with a penis. Further, there is something about the vibe and energy of a lesbian that is desperately attractive to me. I had only been born a woman I would have had 10 TIMES as much pussy as I have actually gotten in this lifetime. The simple fact is that I can't get laid because I have a penis. It's okay, though, because *I fuck animals!* And that goat over there is looking pretty fucking sexy to me right about now!

## Used Toilet Paper

Wal-mart will accept almost anything as returned merchandise. However, there are certain things that you simply should not try to return for a refund. You might get away with, "This blender doesn't work right.", but some items, *toilet paper* comes to mind, simply should not be returned. What are you going to do? Walk up to the counter with a garbage bag full of USED toilet paper and say, "It wasn't soft enough." And expect a refund? Do you think that they can sell it to the next customer? Well, maybe they could in Iowa…

## New and Improved

You know what pisses me off? When they advertise something as being NEW *and* IMPROVED! If something is new, then you don't have a basis for comparison as to how it USED to be, so it by definition cannot be improved. If on the other hand it *is* improved, then we must assume that there was a previous version of it, therefore it is NOT *new*! Most advertisement is based upon first retarding you, then manipulating you into buying a product or service that you neither want nor need. The whole "New and Improved" line was designed to reduce your level of intelligence and consciousness. They have thousands of mechanisms that are designed merely to make you a better, more cooperative and retarded slave.

### Burning *fat* on both ends

I find the term "burning the candle at both ends" interesting. Have you ever thought about what that means? It makes no sense that a person would burn both ends of a candle at the same time. I mean, think about it. When I was a child, I thought about lighting two end of a candle, and it made no fucking sense to me. There is no practical advantage in performing such an act. How that term originated is this: A person who works long and hard hours often got up and started working before the sun was up, necessitating the use of a candle. Someone who worked long and hard as they could would also have to burn a candle after the sun had gone down. Therefore, "burning a candle at both ends" meant at both ends of the *day*, not both ends of the *candle*.

Now let's envision a scenario where a person works physically hard before then sun rises until after the sun goes down. Can we say that such a person burns fat at both ends?

## Wedding Crap

At some time in history, I am sure that there has been a bride who crapped herself during her wedding ceremony. Maybe it was something she ate, or an after-effect from something she did at the party with her friends, but I am sure there has been a bride somewhere in history who suddenly realized that WHITE was not the best choice for the color of the wedding dress. Perhaps brown would have attracted less attention...

## Kitty Cat Liposuction

I have a fat cat. In fact, she is really fucking fat! This kitty cat weighs over 18 pounds, and that is really huge for a cat. It makes me want to take her to one of those new pet spas. You know, the ones where you can pay a pet masseuse to massage your cat, but you have to bribe him with some pussy. On the other hand, if he massages her a little bit lower, maybe you should charge for instead of pay for the service. I hear that these days they now have clinics where you can get your pet liposuction... What kind of a culture have we become in which we now have *pet liposuction?*

### Flying Farts

Where did the term, "let one fly" come from? It is likely it had to do with archery. Now, what if you were shooting farts instead of arrows? If someone you don't like is annoying you, can you "let one fly" and get them to back off at bit? And if you became a master of defensive farting, would they consider you a "martial fartist?"

### Kim Chi

For those of you who don't know this, Kim Chi is the national food of Korea. It also has many beneficial properties, including being an antibiotic (because of the garlic), it has many beneficial bacteria that your body needs, it has anti-carcinogenic properties, it has anti-heart disease properties, and it has anti-aging properties as well! Unless someone murders you, if you eat Kim Chi, it is likely that you will die of old age! On the other hand, there is so much garlic in it that you are likely to not have very many friends!

## Iowan Corn (Holing)

Iowa is well known as the corn-holing capital of the world. There are more people fucking an asshole at any given moment in Iowa than anywhere else on the planet. You know when you are fucking your girlfriend's asshole and you realize that you feel… something else… in there? You know what I mean. You get the sensory feedback that you dick is not alone in that butt. The result can be an "Ice cream cock" situation. When you pull your dick out, there is a lump of shit stuck on top of it like a scoop of ice cream on top of an ice cream cone.

## Human Baby Birthing

This is a true story: The other day I woke up and there was a turd in the bed behind me. No, not someone who I slept with but literally an actual turd! I figured out what I was doing wrong; I was sleeping in the fecal position. You know what the "fecal position" is, right? It's like when a person is curled up with his knees and legs up against his chest, and his arms curled in, like a little baby boy crappin' in his mother's wound.

This got me to thinking. When a baby is just a couple of weeks from being born, does it know about going to the bathroom? Or does it just shit right there inside its mother? I think that this is why when an infant is born there is a bunch of shit that gushes out of the mother following the baby. It has been in there shitting for months. So I conclude that there are times when a woman has a crap-filled vagina. This does explain some things.

It now makes sense to me that at one point my mother had a crap-filled vagina. This explains my sister. Her entire life, my sister has always smelled of two things: horrible body odor and the smell of shit! But seriously, have you ever met my sister; have you ever *smelled* her?

### Fetal Lesbians

You know that many people just have a strong sense of their sexuality even when they are very young. What if there was a baby girl who before birth just had a very strong feeling that she will always want to make love with other girls? Would the event of her birth become a sexual experience for her? Would she be turned on by being inside a woman's vagina as she was on the way out? And as her head emerged from her momma's vagina, might her first act in life be to lick her mother's clitoris?

## Detachable Dicks

Every man at some point has wished that he could detach his dick and send it over to a sexy woman, hoping that it will do a better job seducing her than he could.

So let's follow that scenario as though it could actually happen.

Your dick manages to crawl up to a very beautiful woman and put on its most alluring face. It tries to look cute and adorable.

Now how does *she* react? "Oh, it's so cute!" Her friend says, "It looks hungry. Don't feed it; it'll follow your home!"

She decides to pet it, and comments, "I think it is crying." Her petting made it throw up. Maybe she should kiss it and see if it turns into a prince...

## Bestial Necrophiliacs

I have heard of people who fuck non-human animals, and I have heard of people fucking dead people. But are there people who get turned on at the thought of fucking dead animals? Does a bestial necrophiliac get aroused when he sees a dead donkey on the side of the road, and think, "I'd like a piece of that ass!" What does he think if he sees a dead fox? "Heck, there's a sweet piece of tail!"

## Bathrooms

Let's say that you are working outside in your garden when you realize that you have an anal emergency on your hands. You have to shit, and right now, it feels like diarrhea. You drop your trowel and run for the house. Unfortunately, when you get there, the door is locked. You pull out your keys as fast as you can. Nature almost always has a way of fucking you over, and in this sad little situation, you drop your keys. Well, your ass is about to explode, and you can't get through a locked door, so in a big hurry, you bend over to pick up your keys. Right at that moment, nature plays another trick on you and you get one of these massive convulsion sneezes that you don't get any warning about... You then realize why they put a shower right next to the toilet. You have to peel off all of your clothing, and after evacuating your bowels, you definitely will want to jump into the shower! It is not such a big deal, because when you live on a farm, you sometimes get covered in shit, and it is necessary to take a shower to get clean. After all, every waste-water related facility is attached to the *same* sewer line, right? The sink, toilet, and shower might appear to drain in different places, but right under your floor they are all attached to the same sewage line. So ultimately, it doesn't matter if you have to wash shit down your shower drain; it all is the same in the end. It is not considered appropriate etiquette, but if you crap in the shower instead of the toilet, it doesn't do any harm as long as you can wash it all down the drain. For instance, if you crap in the shower and it is a hard firm turd, you can always pick it up and drop it into the toilet, and then wash your hands. On the other hand, if you have a really runny BM, it will all just wash straight down the drain with no additional effort. The problem comes in when you drop a poop in the shower that is too soft to pick up, but it won't wash down all by itself. You have to sort of push it with your fingers down the drain. This is when you get an education in what the human digestive system actually processes, and what just passes through. You will never find a bit of meat that is undigested. On the other hand, you will find undigested pieces of mushrooms, olives, onions, celery, peppers, eggplant, broccoli, lettuce, cauliflower, and of course CORN! It turns out that the human digestive system is amazingly good at digesting and processing meat, but is not designed to deal with vegetables at all. I guess this is why most human vegetarians are so skinny. Their bodies are not able to absorb over 80% of the food that they eat.

### Death or Senility

I live in Iowa, and I have *never* met so many stupid people anywhere else in America! The people in Iowa are so stupid that they are completely unaware of what intelligence is, and that they don't possess any of it.

However, I heard that the state government is thinking about implementing a system of education in Iowa. I don't think it is going to happen, because it is illegal to educate American slaves.

On the other hand, in spite of the fact that Americans in general are stupid as hell, as is most of the human race, there are also smart people out there. But you know something? Some day the smart people will also be stupid. We are *all* stupid at some point in time. If you *are* a smart person, you are facing two possibilities: Either you will die young (which is tragic), or you will some day be senile. Even people who keep most of their intelligence until they are very old lose it in the end, even if it doesn't happen until they are over ninety years old. My mother is 84 years old, and is at that sad stage where she is utterly senile, but doesn't *know* that she is senile. She says bizarre things to me, like, "All Jews are born on the moon". I look at her and have no idea how to respond to statements that have no bearing on reality whatsoever. By the time she has said it, she has forgotten that she said it because her memory retention is now down to just a few seconds. She forgets words *as she is saying them*! Her mind drifts in a thousand directions at a time, and she has no way to organize her thoughts or retain the memory of things that have happened less than one minute ago. She has instantaneous memory erasure, and one of the sad parts of all of this is that when you are senile, you don't remember that you have forgotten that you used to remember what you now forget. In other words, you can't remember what it is that you _used_ to know, so you are not cognizant of previously having more memory, or having forgotten much of it. Everything *seems* normal because you don't remember how much you have forgotten. Here's the worst part: Your LONG TERM memory remains in tact, so you remember every time you have been persecuted, hurt, raped, or tortured in your entire life. In a state of senility, the present is gone, and all you are left with are memories of how painful life has been! Every life ends in a state of constant torment.

There was this one time when I Mom and I were arguing. She called me a "son of a bitch", and I briefly considered arguing that point. Then I realized that I better just let her have that one!

**Pharmacologists**

These days, if you know what you are doing, you can produce better herbal medicinal remedies than those offered by Pfizer. The corporations just want to addict you to their noxious potions. The best anti-carcinogen in the world is shitake mushrooms. The best antibiotic is garlic. The most health-inducing food is Kim Chi. We are now talking about the difference between a farm-ocologist and a pharmacologist!

**Cougars**

Have you seen the kind of man who women on Match dot com are looking for? Even women in their fifties are not interested in dudes over 35 years old. They must have sex and only sex on their minds. A man is made up of more than a dick, but I guess they don't care about wisdom or being well established financially. They are going to end up with a child with no experience sexually or otherwise. They say that a man reaches his sexual peak at about the age of 19. What they don't tell you is that the "peak" is actually a plateau, and that it doesn't go DOWN until you reach your sixties! That means that you have at least twenty years in there where you are desperate to stick your dick into vaginas, but no woman will sleep with you! As you grow older, your ability to maintain a hard on, your knowledge of how to touch a woman to maximize her pleasure and your self-control to make the experience last increase, but as you get better, harder, and longer, women want to avoid you in lieu of eye candy instead! So you Cougars and young women out there can go ahead and fuck children who have no real idea as to how to make love! I have a message to all of the "Cougars" out there: "you made your bed now lie in it! "… Cougars don't want to date a man who is over forty years old. We can temper our desperation with the energy we are holding back. Older men have experience, have *learned* some things, and can *last longer!* An older man knows that this might be the *last* time he ever gets laid, so he is willing to do *anything* to make it a memorable experience and last longer. "You can use an electroshock bull's asshole dildo on my butt; it is okay with me as long as it draws out the experience!"

**Time and Age**

Have you noticed that when you are a very young child, time seems to go by very slowly? If you parents tell you that you can do something in "just a couple of years", it seems like it is going to take forever!

As you grow older, time seems to pass more and more quickly. When you hit your middle ages, years appear to just whip on by! I wonder if a whole year seems to just take a few seconds to someone when they get over 90 years old. And does that mean that when you are dead, the passage of time becomes instantaneous?

## The Universe, Consciousness, and Time

The universe cannot experience movement without time. Physicists like to view time as a function of space, but that it a limited view at best. If time is reduced to a value of 0, then we still have space, mass, and existence, but nothing would ever happen. No movement would occur. If you reduce time to 0, which happens in a black hole or at any point where you can accelerate mass or space to infinity, then the movement of the universe stops. Time becomes a point. On the other hand, if you can accelerate time to infinity, then the universe ends. The existence of the universe is dependent upon time. Outside the universe, there is a similar relationship between time and consciousness.

Outside of our universe of three large dimension of space, you can view consciousness as time and time as space. Outside the universe, any movement in time is dependent upon consciousness. The way reality works is that space and mass can experience no movement without time, and time cannot experience movement without consciousness. Ultimately, consciousness creates and moves the entire universe, multiverse, and omniverse. Our consciousness itself creates everything around us, and everything we experience.

### The Bunny Olympics

One would think that while the winter is wearing on, one's gardens would be pretty much safe and time-warped until spring. This is *not* the case. For one thing, you can't really weed in winter in this hemisphere, but if you let the weeds grow until spring, you are going to have one hell of a weeding job before you can plant again!

It is said that if you build a better idiot-proof system, then someone will invent a better idiot. The same thing goes for rabbits. I built a 24" fence around my gardens in an attempt to keep the bunnies out. As it turns out, all through the winter they bunnies were practicing long jump and high jump, and anything that could get them over and past a 24" fence.

That's right, they were holding the Bunny Winter Olympics, and the Gold Metal winners got to eat my spring garden!

## Killing Butterflies

I have become a butterfly killer. That seems mean at first, but there is logic behind it. When I see a butterfly in one of my greenhouses, I smash it immediately. If one sees a butterfly "innocently" drinking some dew of the leaf of a broccoli plant, for instance, it doesn't appear at first to be doing any harm. What you DON'T see is that it is swinging its posterior underneath the leaf, and depositing eggs. Eventually, the eggs will hatch out and the larvae will proceed to devour the plant. Not only are they eating a plant that is a food resource for me, but they also shit all over the plant. Have you ever heard the expression "don't shit where you eat"? Well, I have a saying too: Don't shit where *I* eat, you little wormy motherfuckers!

# Chapter 7: Stories

### Hillary Clinton Dream

Here is a really bizarre dream that I actually had. I was invited to a political party supporting Democratic candidates. I got to meet Hilary, and I was really glad because I have great respect for her. Apparently, I am attracted to her too, because we kissed, and in a sexually explicit manner. Here is where it gets weird: Hillary was (in my dream) *not* married to Bill, but rather her husband was George W Bush! (I know, it's fucked up) Hillary and I made out, tongues included, and after that her husband sent out a hit squad to kill me because of what I had done. In the dream, I killed the hit men, but WTF; it was only a dream after all.

### Drunken Parents

My parents were coming home from a party drunk as fuck, and Dad had to pee. He held it as long as he could, then told Ma that he couldn't hold it anymore, and was not going to be able to make it home to get to a bathroom. They noticed a row of trees on the lawn next to the street where they were driving, and concluded it was a park, so Dad got out and pissed on one of the trees. He got back in the car and started driving again, when they were surprised to find that they were home in just a few seconds. The next morning they got up and realized that in his drunken state, Dad had peed in the neighbor's yard!

**Broken Arm**

This is an utterly true story. I almost earned my own Darwin award when I cut the end off of a tree branch with a chainsaw. I had the ladder I was on leaning up against the branch, not thinking about the fact that it was the weight of the portion of the branch that I was cutting off which held the rest of the branch down, which is what provided the support for the ladder I was on… Do you see where this is going? I cut through the portion of the branch which I was removing, and the base of the branch snapped up several inches, because it was no longer being held down by the weight of the end of the limb. It snapped up so far that it was no longer supporting the ladder. I was then at the top of a ladder, about 20 feet up, with a running chain saw, and had NOTHING supporting the ladder. HELLO? I and the chainsaw fell as the ladder went down. In retrospect, I was actually very lucky. I think that I had the wind knocked out of me, but picked myself up pretty quickly. However, from the angle that my left hand was hanging off of the wrist, it was obvious that I had broken that arm.

I didn't panic, but I walked back to the house and went inside and called my mother for a ride to the hospital. She said that she was in the middle of teaching a music lesson, and besides, her car was at the mechanic's repair garage getting some work done.

Well, she sent her student home and used her sister's car to come and pick me up. I was injured and not in the mood to wait for them, so I just started walking in the direction in which they would be coming. I have a 132 pound Great White Pyrenees dog named "Strider", and he was walking by my side. When Ma and Esther finally arrived, they *drove right past me!* After all, it might have been some *other* man about my height and weight and *my* face cradling a broken arm who *happens* to be accompanied by an enormous white dog, right? You see that all the time on a dirt road that *never* has pedestrians, right? Fuckin' shit! How fucking retarded can a person get?

So I finally got to the hospital and these retards explained that the have NO idea as to how to treat an injured person! They threw a splint on my arm and explained that I have to wait until Monday and have an appointment with a REAL doctor, because their "emergency service" has no ability to help someone who is hurt! Jesus fucking Iowans! Fuck!

# Chapter 8: Weird Trips

Humans are the only animals who try to change their gender! I mean, is this part of nature? Why is it that there are millions of species of life on this planet, and yet the only ones who try to change their gender is *Homo sapiens sapiens*?

OF COURSE I offend myself! EVERYONE offends me!

"If oil is the BLOOD of Satan, then money is its seed!"

Did you notice how wet the local water is today? It just seems particularly wet and drippy to me. Try this: Rinse a plate or glass in your sink water. Then hold it up and watch the water drip off. See? It is far drippier than usual.

Is ice like vegetables? Do I have to boil it before I put it in the freezer?

My wife and I just had a baby. When I tell people this, they usually ask if it is a boy or a girl. I tell them, neither one. Our baby is a celibate omnisexual androgynous transgender hopeful.

I'm a pre-operative tranny. I decided to not go through with the final procedure. My theme is: "This dong remains the same."

What if a clitoris was a neurological map of the female body? Could you lick her tits ON her clit?

Have you ever heard of a "Fart Restaurant"? It is a public smelling establishment where people can go to enjoy the kinds of farts they most like to smell. When you arrive, they will ask you what section you want to be seated in. Depending on the scent of the farts you like, based on cuisine, of course, you can be seated in Mexican, Indian, Italian, French, or the American breakfast section. The American breakfast section is heavy on ham and egg farts. When you are seated in a particular section, you can order from the specified cuisine. You can also tip the waiter, who has been fed on the chosen cuisine, to fart in your face for you! You can experience the heavily cumin and chili - laden fart from a Mexican waiter, for instance. After you have eaten and spent some time in the Fart Restaurant, you will start to produce the farts that you enjoy yourself. It is a very rewarding experience! Gay guys go there, because the scent of a fart reminds them of their lover's ass.

I lost my wife five years ago. It wasn't easy! Had to divorce her to get rid of her ugly ass!

A buddy of mine and I were just leaving to go out to a club when he said he wanted to get his, "dikwette". I had no idea what a *dikwette* is, so I asked him, "You mean before we leave? Well, hurry up and get it."

What do you mean, Dad? I don't even HAVE a pregnant wife to kick in the stomach!

There's nothing more evil in this world than a book. Books force people to read, which causes brainwashing. Using writing to manipulate a person's consciousness is a totally evil thing to do. Never read a book!

When someone tries to censor my speech, I tell them, "I will fist-fuck you, and then fuck your kids with your hard-on!"

If a virgin squeezes out a shit, and it is alive, does she say, "Holy shit!"?

My cats shit in my underwear. They have a rule that they can shit anywhere I do.

The "McFreedom" - ground human meat hamburger for the Chinese, made from 100% High Fructose Corn Poison fed American slave!

Here is a weird trip: My cousin Ray stuck is cock in his daughter's anal orifice, and now says that he is not going to take it out until she is 40! I am sorry, but I don't even find this funny, but it is freaky. What if the world *is* destroyed in 2012? His daughter, his little girl, is going to be *anally raped* by her own father for the *rest of her life!*

Laws don't seem to apply equally to everyone. Should laws apply to both humans and automatons? I mean, can a robot be found to be guilty as charged?

Am I outgoing? Heck yes! I am Gregorian.

Hey, if it was ever going to be later, then it would be later now.

You know how dogs and cats like to sniff each other's buttholes? Well, my pets think sniffing my fingers is close enough...

Babies are poo; have you ever seen one coming out?

The word "baby" translates as "food" in most of the animal kingdom. (What the FUCK do you THINK that the dingo was going to do with your baby? Return it after giving it a bath?)

You know how guys can always see through the clothing of a sexy woman? Well, hiney sight is always 20/20.

Chickens get a certain expression on their faces when they are contemplating laying an egg. It's like when you are looking at someone and you can tell from their expression that they are contemplating a shit…

I think that my dick is a ventriloquist. When I am with a beautiful woman, it makes me say the most outlandish things!

Cats HATE soy sauce. I think that this is because there are places where people put soy sauce on cat meat.

Yea, your cock can get hungry. You get nowhere by feeding your tummy when it is your dick that needs feeding. On the other hand, if you can get your hands on some food, maybe a woman will be willing to feed some pussy to your dick. I think that men and women have been doing it like this for tens of thousands of years: "Hey I killed a deer with my spear. Suck my dick?" That's why so many weapons resemble penises. When a man is out there trying to kill something, it is his dick he is trying to feed, not just the tribe.

People who don't know me HATE me. On the other hand, people who get to know me *despise* me. That's how I can tell who my friends are.

God had a sense of humor – guys look ridiculous. Women are a feat of engineering.

A commercial said, "...circle like the sun and the moon..." Have we completely forgotten astrophysics?

Someone somewhere at some point in time has used HUMAN INTESTINES as sausage casings!

My cat was spraying everywhere inside and outside the house. I realized he is saving me a fortune in cat litter!

Viagra? If you do BLUE you've the DEVIL in you!

I am not sure what a "mature audience" is; I'm not one.

Women's hormonal fluctuations - it's not you; it's the thing you fucked last night!

If you refer to a woman as being female in any way while she is acting badly due to a hormonal imbalance, it is always an insult.

If you let a turd nurse on your nipple, you
can raise a republican. Or an accountant...

Last Thanksgiving, I gave some turkey to
my cats. They passed right out. Every one of
them was out cold, and they didn't even help
me with the dishes!

# Chapter 9: Political Jokes

I hear that Ru Paul is running for president. His slogan is:" Transform America!"

If Obama had a Dirty Sanchez, how would you know?

"Democracy is an Obama Nation"
- George W. Bush, 2008

Can everyone hear Obama's sin, or should Obama's Sin Louden?

If John McBush and Barrack O'Busha were to run against each other again, would Bush still be the wiener?

I call him President Obama, but George W. Bush just calls him "Toby".

Satan's Marionette (the "President") isn't even able to move its own bowels. I don't know what technology they use, but I am sure that Shell Oil makes him go in the morning.

There is a *whore* who is running for President in 2012. She is running for the Teabag Party, but I think that she is definitely a member of the *Bush* family!

# Chapter 10: Christian & Religious Jokes

## Not another Disclaimer!?

If you are a conservative fundamentalist Christian, you DO NOT have a sense of humor. Put this book down immediately! The following jokes are intended to offend Christians by design. I also take a shot at virtually every major religion. ☺ If you cannot laugh at your own religion (or someone else's), then go no further.

A good Christian waits his whole life to meet God. When he enters the Pearly Gates of Heaven, he is given a number and told that he can meet God and ask him one question when his number comes up in the queue. He stands in line behind a long line of people waiting to meet God. When his number comes up, he comes before God. God asks him, "What can I do for you my child?" The Christian pulls out a blade and slices God's throat open! Blood spews out in every direction! As the light begins to fade from God's eyes, the Christian says, "Forgive me, Father, for I have sinned."

Question: Why are there so many Christians on Earth?

Answer: Because their souls were kicked out of Heaven.

Question: Why do Christians want so badly to go to Heaven?
Answer: Because they want to destroy it.

Question: Why did Jesus Christ cross the road?
Answer: He was going to go see The Aristocrats.

People who spend a lot of time together tend to look more alike over time.
I associate with Christians, so over time I look increasingly like a rooster.

Well I wouldn't call him a cook per se, but I have heard that Jesus tosses a mean salad!

What does the meat of a human child taste like? I don't know - ask a Christian!

The Virgin Mary might have been a virgin, but I know for a fact that she did have a dick in her vagina at least once. No one is claiming that Jesus was born through cesarean section, right? So at least briefly, she did have a dick in her: Jesus' dick!

Jesus never *did* have a mustache; he just wore a Dirty Sanchez.

So this Jehovahs Witness goes up to a big house and rings the doorbell. He waits a bit and the door opens. Jesus Christ answers the door...

I knew Jesus Christ personally, and he was *no virgin!* He knew that he was the son of God, and he used it to get laid all the time. He would tell sluts, "Hey, want to blow me and get instantly forgiven?" It worked every time!

Think about this: I am sure that more than a few sluts have bribed their way past the pearly gates by sucking cock! Why the FUCK do you think they call him "St. *Peter"?* And why are the gates *"pearly"*? <Author's sidebar: Christians are *such* cocksuckers! What they don't know is that this is the *only* way to get into Heaven!> Additional Sidenote: *"Pearly Gates"* is also a nick-name for Microsoft's Bill Gates. Want to guess why? LOL!

No one hates Christians as much as Jesus! That's because they just spent two thousand years doing what Jesus asked them to *not* do!

The Gods of all religions get together for their annual orgy. Jesus, as usual, shows up early because he wants to be the first to get a piece of Buddha's big fat cock. Krishna arrives on the scene and sticks a finger up both of their butts, then proceeds to go down in sixty-nine position with Shiva, and they suck each other's cocks. Allah, Jehovah, and Yahweh all start sucking each other's dicks, which if you know anything about religion, they are actually all the *same* god! That means that this god is actually sucking his own cock, but then what is the point of being omnipotent, if you can't blow yourself? Buddha's sperm is now dripping down Jesus' face, and Jesus starts to suck God's dick. Right then, Satan pops into the party and shoves is penis right up Jesus' asshole! As Jesus takes it in the mouth and butt simultaneously from God and Satan, Krishna performs his "multiple dicks" trick and fucks all of the other gods in the mouth and ass at the same time, expanding as necessary to completely fill every orifice! Jesus starts eating Satan's asshole, and smears some shit on his upper lip. Then Ganesh lumbers into the orgy, and all the gods scatter, except for Jesus who was so distracted slurping down Satan's shit that he didn't see him coming, and Ganesh shoves his trunk straight up his ass, giving it a godly stretching! A good time was had by all, and the all-god sex orgy was considered a raving success!

How can you tell a Christian? He's got shit on his face and he's sucking a cock!

A wise man once said to God, "The only one NOT doing his job around here is YOU!" I have to say to God, "DON'T think that you are tossing me a bone if *all you are doing is tossing me a bone!*"

Jesus was a fecalphiliac. He liked shit inside of people. He liked shit coming out of people, and he loved playing in shit after it has been excreted. The history books have a tendency to avoid this historic fact. Jesus has the annoying tendency to forgive humans (and this gives you a solid foundation for this tendency), but he also loved to bathe himself in the shit (and bad karma) of humans. Jesus didn't just die for humanity's sins; he died for the shit pouring from their collective ass! Jesus was a fucking idiot. There is no way to justify the behavior of someone who likes being covered in human shit.

So this Christian walks into a bar with a limping monkey.
Christian to Bartender: "I don't get it; they say that monkeys *like* bananas."
Bartender: "Hmmm. That is strange. I don't get it either. What can I get for you?"
Christian: "A banana and a jar of Vaseline, please - and a shot of whisky for me!"

When Jesus shits, do his feces come out with little halos on them?

71

# Chapter 11: Old Jokes

<Here are a few jokes which I made up a long time ago>

## Iowan... Women?

I am *not* saying that all Iowan farmers are into bestiality. I mean, have you seen their freaking wives? What I am saying is that if you have seen Iowan women, who can really tell the difference? If an Iowan farmer's wife catches him screwing a sow, does she get jealous, or does she realize that he made a totally understandable and legitimate mistake?

## The Yorky

A woman was walking her Yorkshire terrier when two thugs walked up to her and demanded that she fork over her money. With one foot under the dog and a yank on the leash, she whipped the dog up into her arms and spun it around to point its ass at the attackers. With one hand she raised its stump of a tail and yelled: "This Yorky Is loaded; and I know how to use it!

## Doughnut Land?

There's something about the name "Doughnutland" that makes me want to immigrate. ;)

## Fini-shit yourself yolks

<I once invented a genre of joke in which the comedian would provide a set-up, and the audience is expected to think up a punch line of their own.>

Question: What did the manure connoisseur say?
Answer 1: Waiter! There is a fly on my shit!
Answer 2: I said that I want the corn *on the side!*
Answer 3: <Provide yourself>

Question: How many electrons does it take to screw in a light bulb?
Answer 1: None. It is impossible. Electrons have no mass.
Answer 2: Two. But they prefer to go to a motel.
Answer 3: <Provide yourself>

# Chapter 12: Rants

## Vegans

You know one thing that I FUCING HATE in this world? VEGANS! I hate vegans so much that I would gladly beat one to death with a large squash, one that I probably got from my own garden. Why? Vegans are fucking yuppies! Vegetarians, on the other hand, are hippies.

Vegans say the word, "vaca", where vegetarians say the word, "vacation". A vegan will say, "ASAP", where a vegetarian would just say, "as soon as possible". Vegans are fucking lazy shit-bags.

A vegan will drive to the whole foods store while using its cellular phone, and drive over a kid on the way there and is not even aware of the act. A vegetarian, on the other hand, will walk to the farmer's market and buy bulk ingredients to make food from scratch. A vegetarian doesn't even have a cell phone, because he is in tune with nature.

A vegetarian has a garden and grows and cooks the best organic food imaginable. He eats peppers, cabbages, egg plant, collards, chard, kale, squash, pumpkins, cucumbers, lettuce, and tomatoes.

A vegan, on the other hand, can't even fucking cook. He is a fucking *junkatarian* - he is a nasty *carbivore* who eats pies, cakes, cookies, candy, chocolate, ice cream, tarts, trifle, turnovers, chips, soda pop, fruit juices, grains, bread, biscuits, muffins, peas, potatoes, carrots, and corn! All junk food! A VEGAN is a fucking disgusting CARBOHOLIC!

Vegetarians are intelligent and educated, and are producers in the culture. Vegans, on the other hand, are worthless filthy yuppie consumer scum!

If you are too weak physically or psychically too actually *say* the word "vegetarian", then EAT SOME FUCKING MEAT!!!

## American Pundits

I am not accustomed to thinking that Wikipedia is wrong, but I looked up their definition of "pundit", and they were completely wrong historically, culturally, and in every possible way. The word "pundit", as well as "guru" "yagya", and "jyotishee" all come from the Indian culture (that is, from Asia, for the idiots out there).

Americans cannot ever be pundits, because they are not celibate, vegetarian, Indian boys who are trained in advanced mental techniques such as yagyas. Americans are just using the word "pundit" incorrectly because they are retarded and are collectively on a national ego trip. One cannot ever have a "political pundit" because a *true* pundit by definition would never concern himself with politics. Real pundits do not predict the future; that job is left to a jyotishee. The pundit's job is to *change* the future by performing a yagya. American culture since the year 2000 has become such a piece of shit that I cannot (as hard as a try) put it into words! This is one of the little things that just *PISSES ME OFF!* The billionaire scumbags think that they can dictate what culture is, packaged and sold to retards, where what they are actually producing is UTTER SHIT!

### Never Say "I love you" to a woman

There are certain words that can pass between two people that spell the death of a potential relationship before it has gotten started. Every man knows *exactly* what I am talking about here. If a woman ever says, "You're such a good friend", the man knows that he will never get a piece of that ass. This woman will never have sex with him, will not marry him, and will not have children with him. When a man hears these words from a woman whom he loves, it feels (that is, actually *physically feels*) like a dagger being shoved into his heart (which is attached to his dick, of course.)

The other thing that can kill a relationship is if the man doesn't know when to say "I love you" to the woman. It is actually a very simple rule, and all men must adhere to it, or accept that he will never get laid.

To all male readers: First, decide whether you have inserted your penis into the vagina of the woman who you like. If the answer is NO, then definitely DO NOT say the words "I love you" to her. If you do, then she will never grant you access to her vagina. I know this sounds strange, but it does appear to be consistently true. If you truly DO want to insert your penis into her vagina, then you may make conversation with her as you will, but AVOID these three words, or you will have to seek a mating relationship with another female.

On the other hand, if you *have* inserted your penis into her vagina, then it is a good and appropriate time to say the words "I love you" to her. Point of fact, many women will expect or even insist upon you saying "I love you" to her *after* you have engaged in sexual intercourse with her.

If you are currently in the process of inserting your penis into a woman's vagina as you are reading this, then you now have permission to say "I love you" to her, but she will probably not take you very seriously, because every man feels that way when he is in the process of having an orgasm with his penis inserted in a vagina.

### Black Friday Idiot Consumer Niggahs!

Fuck! This really nauseates me - I heard a bit on the radio that said that thousands of Missourians were lining up for Black Friday deals! My fucking God in Hell! FUCK CHRIST! Missouri is one of the five stupidest states in the union. We now can see these brain-dead consumers lining up to spend money they don't have on shit that they neither need or want, just to GIVE IT AWAY! Why don't you just line them all up and shoot them? Americans are totally brainwashed into spending their money to get some freaking "Savings". If you are *spending* your money, it isn't a savings. Try *not* being a consumerist dick. That'll save you some money.

My idea of gift giving involves giving honey, or pickles, or some other kind of food grown and made on my farm. It is cheaper, it is better quality than the fucking *crap* made by the corporations, and it is more meaningful, symbolically.

Everything that I am giving to family on Christmas is either food, or a tool used to make food. Buying fucking crap to give away is something that a fuck-head vegan on "vaca" would do. A vegetarian, on the other hand, would make a macramé or some candles with wax from his own hives, and give that to someone he loves. Do you know why they call it "Black" Friday? Because you are all consumerist fucking NIGGERS! It doesn't matter what color your skin is; nor does it matter what your ancestry is. Since the illegal takeover of the Federal government of the USA in the year 2000, Texan oil-rich billionaires from the Confederated States of America have run this country LIKE SHIT, and made every one of you fucking idiots into a Nigger! You are slaves, and you are consumer retards.

### "Went Viral"

I am not against slang in general, and I use and like quite a bit of it, but I can tell when something is not legit slang, but rather something created by a billionaire scumbag. A big part of selling modern day technology to the slave class of the world is getting them addicted to it.

If this term were even legitimately invented by actual people, then it would be okay, but the billionaires play an evil little game with each other whereby they introduce trends into culture, their slave class, and see how many retarded, idiot slaves they can brainwash. Whoever brainwashes the most slaves wins the game.

Terminology should be taken similarly to technology. Never accept anything until you have observed and studied it for at least a couple of years. You know; see how it does in culture. See how it survives and mutates. If it becomes evil or dies, then *don't* invest your money or effort into it.

*Don't* go off buying or saying something until you know whether it is malignant somehow. If you want to say the words, "went viral" or listen to Justin Beiber music, then FUC K YOU! This little piece of brainwashing is intended, among other things, to reduce your level of intelligence and consciousness. It is designed to blur the relationship between a computer virus and an internet-cultural phenomenon.

It is almost always a mistake to *automatically* accept anything that the culture or the billionaire/corporation's pseudo-culture offers.

One could just as easily say, "Became popular" as opposed to "went viral", but some pile of *shit* wanted to see how many of you are completely retarded, so this term was introduced into pseudo-culture. If a person *ever* uses this term seriously in any context other than to disparage it, then you know that that person's brain no longer functions. This is a person who had the opportunity to either use proper English, or perhaps even invent a term of his own, but NO! He (or she) had to use a term supplied by the worst, filthiest, and most evil source available.

I suggest this to you: if you *have* to use a new term, then INFUCKINGVENT ONE YOURSELF! Note that just in writing this book, I have coined at least five new terms myself: "junkatarian", "carbivore", "carbaholic", "pseudo-culture", and "infuckingvent".

If you are the kind of uncreative shit-hole who can't even invent their *own* terminology, then you deserve to burn in Hell, you "went viral" cumsucking fuckhole!

### The American Advertising Industry

The American Advertising Industry is totally evil. They are the incarnation of

Satan itself. Don't even take my word for it. See it for yourself.

Watch the advertisements that your kid sees on TV. Now interpret the visual effects that you see during food commercial advertisements with a Freudian interpretation. What do you see? You see images of penises going into a child's mouth. The advertising industry uses sexuality as a tool to brainwash your children into buying food laced with High Fructose Corn Poison, to which they are addicted. If you are retarded, you will go with it and go buy your kids some Pepsi or some Twinkies.

Try to wrap your brain around the fact that most of the Gangster International Billionaire Terrorist Mobster Organization (GITMO) makes a huge amount of money on war profiteering, and that their corporations, which are used as tools to destroy democracy and our rights, cannot survive without the advertising industry.

You and your children are brainwashed by advertisement so that monsters can blow the arms and legs off of innocent children for the purpose of making money.

**Justin Beiber's Hood**

One of the worst things that I have witnessed in my life is the destruction of the arts, including the art of music. The billionaires, with their approach to computer automation and manufacturing, have gone out of their way to destroy culture for their own evil profit.

You can almost smell the evil of the Texan oil-rich billionaires seeping into what used to be our culture. Whenever these evil fuckers touch ANYTHING, it turns to poison. I used to have the opportunity to enjoy music with creativity and integrity back when The Mothers of Invention was a band who people listened to.

What we know as popular music has died a sad death. GITMO, with their corporations has attacked and destroyed the quality of music in culture with their creation of The New Kids on the Block, NSYNC, The Backdoor Boys (buttwhores), Britney Spears, and Justin Fucking Beiber! These are celebrity images with no real people behind them. Their characters have no talent in terms of musical creativity. They have no ability to play an instrument, or to compose music. Their music and their backup bands are generated by computer. One can be a "star" these days and have no talent whatsoever, just an image. It is totally *fucking* sad!

And what is with this "head partially covered" by a hood fucking look anyway? I mean *really!* If the fucking little idiot *is* a gang-member, then how the fuck did he get to be some sort of oil-sponsored celebrity? On the other hand if he *is* some sort of artificially created millionaire non-musical "artist", why the *fuck* is he sort-of dressed like a member of a freaking street gang? It makes no sense. If he is a gangster, why doesn't he actually COVER HIS HEAD properly and not just *imply* his "gangsterness" and yet go out of his way to SHOW his face?

I am tired of it. PLEASE SOMEONE KILL JUSTIN BEIBER RIGHT NOW!

### Culture VS Pseudo-Culture

America no longer has an actual culture anymore. Society, in other words billionaire corporate lords and Texan oil-rich billionaires now want to commercialize culture and dictate to us what we get to experience as culture. They want to tell you how to speak, what music to enjoy, what to eat, and what technology to be addicted to. What the corporations give us is *not* culture. It is *pseudo*-culture.

What people create for themselves is actual real culture. What you get from the corporations is a plastic covered, shrink-wrapped, mass manufactured, computerized distortion of actual culture. Just remember that these billionaire assholes are evil, and everything they offer is shit.

## Christians Hate Jews

Does it bother anyone that Christians hate Jews? Jews are persecuted and mass-murdered by Christians on a regular basis, and this has been an accepted practice for over a thousand years. Jesus was a Jew. Protestants don't even want to acknowledge that Cathaholics (that's right, there's a CAA too) are Christians, and not only do they base their religion on Jesus Christ, but this is the church which *he* started. But Christians *hate* Jews, except for Jesus. That's right; he is the *only* Jew who they love. I mean, you have to love Jesus Christ, right? After all, he loves you, right? And yet it is acceptable to hate every other Jew on earth or who has ever lived. Christians are fucking idiots, by design. They are lied to and mislead, and their religion has been used to control the masses, and to acquire land, money, power, and slaves since the dark ages. If a Christian comes to my land in the middle of nowhere, I might have to shoot him, but I never see a Buddhist, a Jew, or a Muslim coming to my place to try to convert me. In the world right now, there are at least two billion (retarded) Christians, over one billion Muslims (whom I respect a lot more), and over sixty *million* people who believe in Voodoo! There are now less then 15 million Jews in the world, and one of the reasons for their massive extinction is because of a group of Lutheran Protestant Christians who are widely know as Nazis! They want you to think that socialists murdered millions of Jews, but the spin that you don't hear is that Nazis were also Christian. I mean, who the fuck do you think they were, Muslims? Fuck that! The Nazis were straight up Christians, that gives you the true context for their mass murder of the Jews. On the other hand, Jews have also committed atrocities and caused the extinction of many cultures, and they have proudly documented that historic fact in the Old Testament of the Bible. If you don't believe me, then ask someone from Jericho. But Jesus Christ didn't accept war and mass murder. His message was that people should love each other. Do you really think that he didn't include *his own people* in that philosophy?

www.ingramcontent.com/pod-product-compliance
Lightning Source LLC
Chambersburg PA
CBHW070552030426
42337CB00016B/2454